Table of Contents

All terms appearing in boldfaced type in the text are defined in the Glossary that appears on page 64.

Maria is a ten-year-old **Yanomami** girl. The Yanomami are a tribe of Aboriginal Peoples. They live deep in the tropical rainforest along the Amazon River in South America. Three times each day Maria carries the family water pails down to the river. She takes a few steps into the water to fill the empty pails. Then she walks back to her home. Maria does all this without spilling a drop.

One day Maria went down to the river to fill the pails for her mother as she had done hundreds of times before. She took a few steps into the water. Suddenly she screamed with pain and dropped her pails. Something had bitten her foot.

Maria's mother heard her screams. She came running through the rainforest and pulled Maria out of the water. She carried her up onto the

The Amazon River is located in South America. It begins in the Andes Mountains in Peru and flows through Brazil to the Atlantic Ocean. On its way, the Amazon passes through the largest tropical rainforest in the world.

shore. Maria was crying and her foot was bleeding badly.

What happened was no surprise to Maria's mother. She knew at once that Maria had been bitten by a piranha, one of the most dangerous fish in the world. Many thousands of deadly piranhas live in the Amazon River.

Especially when the water levels of the river are low, groups of piranhas can be hungry and dangerous. They can tear animals and birds apart in no time at all. A school of piranhas can eat a whole cow in five minutes. Their usual prey, however, is other fish, shellfish, or fruits or seeds that fall into the water.

When people fish with nets in the Amazon River, they must be careful. If a piranha is caught in a net, it can bite off a person's finger as clean as if it had been cut off with a knife.

Maria's mother knew that she must get her daughter out of the river quickly. That is why she ran as fast as she could when she heard Maria screaming. She also knew which plants from the rainforest she could use to stop the bleeding and heal the wound.

Maria knew that this time she was lucky. In the rainforest people must always be on the lookout for the dangers that surround them.

Piranhas are small but can be just as dangerous as sharks. Most piranhas are less than 30 cm., but they have rows of razor-sharp teeth and very strong jaws. A piranha can take a nasty bite, but one piranha's bite will not kill a person. The real danger of piranhas is that hundreds of them swim together. When a person or animal wanders into the river, one piranha may take a bite. The bleeding caused by the bite excites the other piranhas. In a few minutes there may be nothing left but a skeleton!

SOMETHING TO DO

1. Draw a picture of the story of Maria. Title your picture "Maria's Lucky Escape."

2. Quiz yourself on piranhas. Do you agree or disagree with these statements? Explain your answers.

   a) Piranhas are large fish.
   b) Piranhas have rows of razor-sharp teeth.
   c) Piranhas mostly swim alone.
   d) Piranhas seldom attack people or large animals.
   e) Piranhas are excited by blood in the water.
   f) Piranhas can be as deadly as sharks.
   g) There are no cures for a piranha bite.
   h) Piranhas can tear their victim apart in a few minutes.
   i) When the river is high, piranhas are most likely to bite.
   j) People fishing must be careful of piranhas caught in the nets.

3. Find out if anyone in your family has a home remedy for a cut, a burn, or a certain illness. Share the remedy with the class.

4. Suppose your canoe overturned on the Amazon River. You manage to swim to shore, but the canoe is lost. You know that it will be 24 hours before anyone else will come by. Choose only three items from the list below that you would like to have to help you survive. Tell why you chose each item.

   knife, shovel, tent, mosquito net, gun and ammunition, rope, six chocolate bars, sunglasses, some bananas, one litre of water, matches, a large sheet of plastic, coat, hat, a package of biscuits.

The Amazon River is the second-longest river in the world. The longest is the Nile River in Africa. The Amazon flows nearly 6500 kilometres across South America. Although the Nile is longer, the Amazon carries more water.

The place where a river begins is called its **source**. The source of the Amazon is high in the west, in the Andes Mountains of Peru. It begins here as hundreds of tiny streams. The streams flow downhill. Eventually they join up and make a river. Later, other streams also join it. The rivers and streams that join the main one are called **tributaries**. As the Amazon flows to the Atlantic ocean in the east, more than 1100 tributaries join it.

The area of land which supplies a river with water is called its drainage **basin**. All the tributaries and the land between them make up the Amazon drainage basin. You can see the Amazon basin and the names of the main tributaries on the map. The basin is the shaded area on the map.

When a river flows into the sea we say it has reached its **mouth**. The mouth of the Amazon at the Atlantic Ocean is more than 320 kilometres wide. From it flows one-fifth of all the fresh water entering the world's oceans. The Amazon also drops a load of **silt** at its mouth. Silt is the sand and other matter that has been washed down by the river on its long journey. Near its mouth the Amazon splits up into several channels. In the middle of the river's mouth is Marajo Island, the largest island in a river in the world. The Amazon empties into the Atlantic Ocean around Marajo Island.

The Amazon River winds for thousands of miles through dense rainforest.

The Amazon River

For several months each year, the Amazon overflows its banks in many places. When this happens, much of the forest along the river bank is covered with water. In lowland areas the water can rise up to 15 metres, twice the height of a two-storey house. In places, the flooding stretches back several kilometres from the main river.

The area that floods regularly is called the **flood plain**. Trees on the flood plain are partly submerged. Fish swim among the lower branches of the trees. People in canoes paddle under the treetops!

People cannot build houses along the Amazon River in the lowland areas where the flood waters are highest. Even in places where the flooding is not so bad, they have to build their houses on stilts. In this way, when the river floods, the houses are not submerged. The water rises to just below the floor boards of the houses. The people inside stay safe and dry.

The Amazon River is a light brown colour. It is full of silt washed down from the soft rocks of the Andes Mountains. Because of its light colour, the Amazon is called the "white" river.

The Rio Negro is the largest tributary of the Amazon. It carries very little silt. For this reason it is darker than the Amazon and is known as the "black" river. When the Rio Negro joins the Amazon, the waters of the two rivers do not mix for about 20 kilometres. They don't mix because the two

rivers have different temperatures. Below is a picture of the Amazon after it has joined with the Rio Negro. Notice the black water from the Rio Negro at the bottom of the photograph.

Find the Rio Negro on the map on page 5. Find where it joins the Amazon River. What is the name of the city where the two rivers meet? In chapter 18 you will find out more about this famous city.

The giant Amazon water lily has huge leaves that grow 1.2 metres across and float on the surface. Each lily pad is strong enough to support a small child.

SOMETHING TO DO

1. Make a simple map of South America. Use an atlas to help you. On your map:

   • Label the Equator, the Atlantic Ocean, the Pacific Ocean, and the Andes Mountains.
   • Draw the Amazon River with a double blue line. Label the Amazon River.
   • Trace the tributaries with a single blue line.
   • Mark and label the cities of Manaus and Belem.
   • Use a dotted line to mark the outline of the Amazon drainage basin. Shade in the Amazon basin green.

2. If you were in a motor boat travelling up the Amazon River from Belem to Manaus, in what direction would you be going?

3. If you were floating down to the mouth of the Amazon with a load of bananas, in what direction would you be going?

4. Many song writers have written about rivers. "Old Man River" and "Shenandoah" are two songs about rivers. Listen to, sing, or read a song about a river. Write your own song about the Amazon River.

DID YOU KNOW?
How the Amazon Got Its Name

The ancient Greeks had a legend about fierce female warriors called Amazons. Legend said these women lived in Asia. In 1542, a Spanish captain named Francisco de Orellana, was sailing down the Amazon. His sailors reported being attacked with bows and arrows by fierce white-skinned women. The Europeans remembered the old Greek legend about the women warriors. They called the river the "Amazon." No evidence has been found that such women ever existed in the rainforest.

here are tropical rainforests in many parts of the world. They are all found inside the **tropical zone**. Three imaginary lines stretch around the earth. The line in the middle of the earth is called the **equator**. North of the equator is a line called the **Tropic of Cancer**. The same distance south of the equator is a line called the **Tropic of Capricorn**. The tropical zone lies between the Tropic of Cancer and the Tropic of Capricorn.

In the tropical zone temperatures are hot all year long because they are close to the equator. There is heavy rainfall almost every day. Forests in these hot, wet areas are called tropical rainforests.

The largest tropical rainforests are found in South America and West Africa. There are also tropical rainforests in South East Asia and parts of northern Australia.

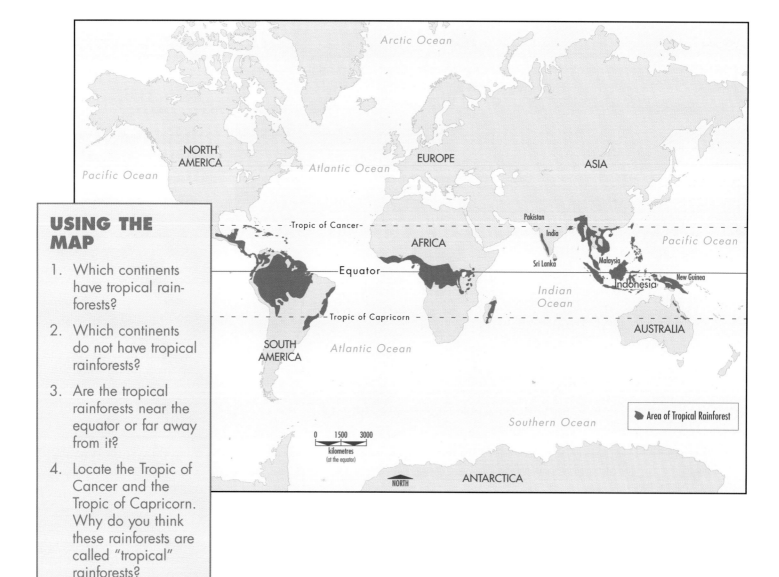

USING THE MAP

1. Which continents have tropical rainforests?

2. Which continents do not have tropical rainforests?

3. Are the tropical rainforests near the equator or far away from it?

4. Locate the Tropic of Cancer and the Tropic of Capricorn. Why do you think these rainforests are called "tropical" rainforests?

THE AMAZON RAINFOREST

The largest tropical rainforest in the world is in South America. This forest is roughly six times the size of Ontario. The Amazon rainforest covers the huge basin drained by the Amazon River and its tributaries. Half the Amazon rainforest is in Brazil. The rest lies in Peru, Bolivia, Columbia, Ecuador, Venezuela, and Guyana.

WHY ARE RAINFORESTS SO IMPORTANT?

Rainforests provide homes for an enormous variety of plants and animals. Over half of the world's **species** or types of plants and animals live in rainforests. Many useful products come from tropical rainforests. They include rubber, Brazil nuts, bananas, coffee, and cocoa. Some of our most valuable timbers like teak, mahogany, and rosewood, also come from tropical rainforests.

Rainforests are also home to thousands of Aboriginal Peoples. These are the people whose ancestors have lived in the rainforest for thousands of years. When Christopher Columbus reached the Americas, he mistakenly thought he had sailed all the way to India. He started calling the people he found

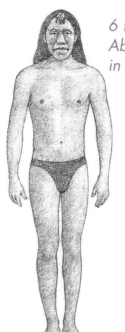

6 to 9 million Aboriginal Peoples in the 1400s.

About 200 000 Aboriginal Peoples in the 1990s.

there Indians. Today we call them Aboriginal Peoples because they were the original inhabitants of these lands.

The Aboriginal Peoples of the rainforest can teach the world important lessons. They can show us how plants and animals of the rainforest can be used for food and medicine.

Rainforests also play a part in helping to control the earth's climate. Rainforests are sometimes called the "lungs of the world." They help us to breathe. Trees make oxygen, which most creatures need in order to live. Rainforests are so huge that they affect the air and the weather everywhere in the world.

Before the arrival of the Europeans, six to nine million Aboriginal Peoples lived in the Amazon Basin. Those numbers have been drastically reduced. Millions of Aboriginals died from diseases brought in by people from other places. Thousands were killed trying to defend their lands. Today, there are probably less than 200 000 Aboriginal Peoples left in the Amazon.

SOMETHING TO DO

1. Draw a shopping cart. Put pictures of rainforest products in the cart. Cut pictures from magazines or draw them. Add to your cart as you read through this book.

2. On an outline map of the world label the Equator and the tropics of Cancer and Capricorn. Label the names of the continents. Shade in the location of the tropical rainforests of the world.

Suppose you went for a walk with Maria in the rainforest. You would find it dark even in the daytime. Most of the trees are **evergreens**. They keep their leaves all year round. Very little sunlight shines through the thick green leaves high above your head.

Huge tree trunks stretch up straight and tall. A typical tropical forest tree is more than 40 metres high. Vines climb the branches and trunks of trees. Some are as thin as string, others are as thick as your arm. They all climb towards the sun.

The air is hot and steamy. It rains almost every day. Mosquitoes are everywhere in the dark, damp rainforest. Brightly coloured birds swoop over your head. You can smell perfume from thousands of flowers. The ground you are walking on feels soft and spongy.

In a way Maria's rainforest is like a very tall office building with many floors or storeys. Each storey is different. Each storey has its own plants and animals living in it. The picture on the opposite page shows the layers or storeys of the rainforest. Compare it with the photo on this page. Try to identify the different layers of the rainforest in the photo.

The Emergent Layer (40 metres to 50 metres)

- a few giant trees with straight trunks break or emerge through the rainforest roof.
- some trees tower 50 metres above the forest floor, making them top heavy.
- the tallest trees often develop **buttress roots** above ground to prop them up and keep them from toppling over.
- trees in the emergent layer get more sunlight.
- trees in this layer are often struck by lightning during storms.

The Canopy Layer (18 metres to 40 metres)

- leaves and branches make a thick green roof.
- the roof of the canopy blocks sunlight out of lower storeys and keeps moisture in.
- trees and branches overlap and form highways for animals to travel along.
- vines climb and twist their way among the trees towards the sunlight.
- orchids and other beautiful flowers cling to the branches of the tall trees.
- most of the rainforest fruit grows here.
- many species of animals, birds, and insects live here.

The Understorey Layer (0 metres to 18 metres)

- extends from near the ground up about 18 metres.
- hardly any sunlight reaches here.
- half-grown trees struggle up to the sunlight.
- shade loving plants, such as some palms, grow here.
- many birds live here.

The Rainforest Floor (0 metres)

- the forest floor is a carpet of dead leaves, ferns, mosses, and mushrooms.
- very little vegetation grows on the forest floor except where sunlight can break through, as along river banks.
- only shade plants with large leaves to absorb the sunlight can grow here.
- buttress roots of tall trees are holding up the trunks as ropes hold up a tent.
- vines begin here and grow up through the layers of the forest.

hink of all the Tarzan movies you have watched. Do you remember how Tarzan comes swinging through the air on a thick woody vine? These vines are called **lianas**. They grow everywhere in the rainforest.

LIANAS—NATURE'S ROPES

Lianas grow out of the forest floor towards the sunlight in the canopy above. To get there they wind around tree trunks or they fasten themselves with tendrils to a young tree in the under-storey. As the young tree grows toward the sunlight, the liana goes along for the ride. Once lianas reach the canopy, they spread out in all directions. Like huge ropes, they loop from branch to branch. They tie together many trees in the canopy. As a result, when one tree falls it may pull others down with it.

EPIPHYTES

Along with lianas, a typical forest tree has other plants growing on it up in the canopy. They are called **epiphytes**. These plants anchor themselves to the trunks and high branches of trees. Epiphytes do not take food or water from the tree. They simply use it as a means of reaching the sunlight. It is estimated that there are roughly 30 000 species of epiphytes in the world's tropical rainforests.

Living high up gives epiphytes the two conditions they need to live. In the canopy they get more sunlight. Also the breezes in the canopy help to spread their seeds. However, they have to find a way to get water in the canopy. Some epiphytes send out aerial roots to draw in water from the moist air. Others catch rainwater using their leaves. This second group of plants is called **bromeliads**.

Lianas grow leaves and flowers in the sunlight of the canopy. They also send down aerial roots to the earth below. Other climbing plants support themselves by attaching to the liana roots. The whole forest is tied together by these woody climbers.

This rainforest tree is covered with bromeliads. The leaves of a bromeliad all join together at the base of the plant. This forms a small water tank that can support different kinds of insect life.

Some Plants of the Rainforest

The problem for plants is getting enough water. Bromeliads have a special way of getting water. They collect water in leaves shaped like containers. The containers or "tanks" form miniature ponds in the treetops. Insects and even frogs lay their eggs in these tanks. Birds and animals visit bromeliads to eat the insects found in the tanks. Monkeys drink water from the tanks.

FLOWERS

Flowers attract birds and bees to the plant. Inside the flower is a yellow powder called pollen. Pollen has to be transferred to other flowers before fruit and seeds will form. Bees and birds carry pollen from one flower to another while they are feeding on the flower's sugary nectar. Bees like brightly coloured flowers with strong perfume. Birds prefer coloured flowers with no scent. Flowers that are white, and open only at night, attract bats and moths.

Some of the most beautiful flowering plants of the rainforest are orchids. Orchids are epiphytes. They piggy-back on branches high in the canopy. About 500 species of orchids have been recorded in the Amazon rainforest.

Pitcher Plant

Certain rainforest plants eat small insects. They are called carnivores meaning they eat meat, in this case, insects. The pitcher plant has flowers shaped like a "jug." Each jug collects rainwater. When the insect enters the jug, the lid snaps shut. The unlucky insect is digested by **enzymes** (chemicals) in the water. It is absorbed into the plant.

The pitcher plant is a meat eater. In the rainforest, there is no shortage of insects to eat!

SOMETHING TO DO

1. Do you remember? What are buttress roots? What are the woody climbing plants called? What are epiphytes? What are plants called that eat insects? What kinds of plants collect water in leaves shaped like "tanks?"

2. As a class activity, plan and make a huge bulletin board display to show the layers of the rainforest. Label the layers. Then cut trees of various sizes, lianas, palm trees, orchids, epiphytes, bromeliads, fruit trees, and other plants, from coloured paper. Add them to your display in the correct layer. Leave room to add more plants and animals to your display as you learn about the rainforest.

3. Mosquitoes carry two deadly diseases. They are malaria and yellow fever. Find out the signs of these diseases.

   - What drugs are used for their cures?

   - Why don't we have these diseases very often in Canada?

   - Why would scientists in the rainforest call the mosquito "Public Enemy Number One?"

You can make a miniature rainforest in your classroom. You will need:
- a glass aquarium and a thermometer,
- a large tray, larger than the top of the aquarium,
- a smaller tray or shallow dish with drainage holes,
- potting soil and sand, and
- plants, such as African violets, small ferns, ivies, and moss.

1. Put some potting soil in the smaller tray. Place the plants close together in the soil. Place a thermometer among the plants.

2. Fill the large tray with damp sand. Place the tray filled with plants on top of the damp sand.

3. Water the plants gently.

4. Place the aquarium upside down over the tray of plants.

5. Put the whole miniature rainforest in a bright place, but not in direct sunlight.

6. Do not water the plants again but make sure the sand is kept damp.

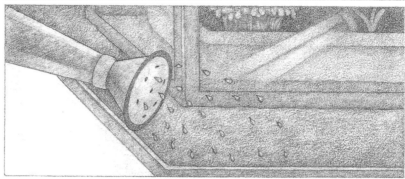

7. Observe what happens in the miniature rainforest.

SOMETHING TO DO

Observe your rainforest and consider:

1. How fast did the plants grow? You could grow the same kinds of plants outside the aquarium and compare their growth.

2. What happens to the inside of the glass aquarium? In a rainforest, clouds often form over the trees during the daytime. Why do you think this happens? Try to borrow a **hygrometer** to measure the amount of moisture in the air. Compare the amount of moisture in the air of your classroom with the amount of moisture inside the miniature rainforest. Also, compare the temperature inside and outside the glass container. What have you learned about the temperature and humidity (amount of moisture) of a tropical rainforest?

3. The glass walls of the aquarium prevent the moisture from escaping. To which layer of the rainforest can the glass be compared?

4. Places where collections of living plants are kept are called botanical gardens. Try to visit a botanical garden. What does it feel like to be in one of the greenhouses where tropical rainforest plants are kept? What is done to create those conditions in the greenhouse? What plants grow in the tropical forest greenhouse?

DID YOU KNOW?

Plants are important to all of us. They feed us, clothe us, and make our air fit to breathe. They help to provide water. They give us materials to build and make things with. They provide medicines for us to take when we are sick. Without plants we could not live.

eaves, fruit, nuts, and seeds are food for many animals. Animals that feed on plants are called **herbivores**.

RAINFOREST BIRDS

Toucans and Macaws

Toucans and macaws are two of the most colourful birds of the

A blue and gold macaw.

rainforest. The toucan has a huge, multi-coloured beak. The beak looks heavy but it is really just a large hollow framework. Toucans are fruit eaters. They gather in flocks of a dozen or more. When they find a tree with ripe fruit, they stand on the strongest branches and reach out with those huge beaks. They grab the juicy fruit and gulp it down. Toucans also use their beaks to toss fruit to each other and hold pretend beak battles.

Macaws are members of the parrot family. A number of species are seen in the canopy of the South American rainforest. They come in a range of bright, beautiful colours: green and red, scarlet, blue and yellow, and other colour combinations. The macaw has a strong curved beak that it uses to crack open nuts.

A toucan in the Amazon.

Rainforest Animals: Plant Eaters

The pacu fish likes to feed on fruit that drops into the Amazon River.

FISH

Believe it or not, there are species of fish in the Amazon that eat fruit. The pacu is one of them. These fish do not have sharp teeth like the piranhas. Instead, their teeth are more like human molars. Their teeth crush, shred, and grind food. When the river floods, there is plenty of food for fruit-eating fish. They swim in the flooded forest and find fruit and seeds that have fallen from the trees. People fishing for pacu bait their hooks with cooking bananas.

BATS

At nightfall many of the animals of the rainforest wake up. We say they are **nocturnal**. These creatures sleep during the day and come out at night. They crawl out of caves and other hiding places to roam and feed at night.

There are over a hundred different species of nocturnal bats in South America. Bats make high-pitched chirps as they swoop through the night air. The echoes from these chirps help the bats to know when they are close to objects. We usually think of bats as eating insects and frogs. But there are also fruit-eating bats in the rainforest. They find fruit with their keen sense of smell.

A fruit bat feeding on the flower of a banana tree.

17

The night monkey of the Amazon is the only nocturnal monkey in the world. At night these monkeys leap among the branches in search of food. Their large forward-pointing eyes help them to see in the dark.

Just before dawn, red howler monkeys set up a noisy chorus. Their piercing screams can be heard a kilometre away. They seem to be warning other monkeys not to come too near. Their cries are also a signal to all the "nightshift" animals to return to their hiding places. The night monkey returns to its home in a hollow tree. Soon the animals of the nightshift will be sound asleep. Another day will begin in the rainforest. Day-time monkeys will come out to play.

MONKEYS

Monkeys have been nick-named the acrobats of the rainforest. They love to swing through the branches of the canopy, high above ground. The monkeys of South America are entirely tree-dwelling. They are well suited to this **habitat** or natural home. Monkeys are excellent climbers. Their tails can be used to grasp things and can wrap around branches like another limb. They leap from tree to tree and scamper along the narrowest branches looking for their favourite foods: fruit, leaves, and birds' eggs. Monkeys are so playful that they will even throw small branches down at intruders to scare them away.

THE SLOTH

One of the most unusual animals of the Amazon rain-forest is the sloth. Unlike monkeys, sloths are very slow moving. They are so slow that it can take a day or so to move from one tree to another. Their top speed is about three metres per minute. Algae often grow in the sloths' fur and give it a green tinge. This makes them hard to see as they hang in trees eating green leaves. Their strong claws lock tightly onto branches and sloths can hang upside down with no fear of falling off. They hang upside down even when fast asleep!

A young three-toed sloth clings to a rainforest tree.

Rainforest Animals: Plant Eaters

LEAF-CUTTER ANTS

Hundreds of species of rainforest insects feed on plants. One of the most common is the leaf-cutter ant. Its sharp scissor-like jaws cut off pieces of leaves. Each ant can carry a piece of leaf several times the size of its own body. In their underground nest ants chew the leaves into a paste. A fungus grows on the paste and the ants live on that fungus. One colony could contain a million ants. A single colony of leaf-cutters can chew several thousand kilograms of leaves each year.

BUTTERFLIES

Millions of butterflies live in each layer of the rainforest. Some are at ground level. They feed on over-ripe fruit that has fallen and is rotting on the forest floor. Others gather around puddles. They drink from the puddles to absorb minerals. Still others flutter in the understorey and canopy. They feed on the nectar of sweet-smelling flowers. There are even nocturnal butterflies that feed on flowers that only bloom at night. More than 2000 species of butterflies live in the Amazon rainforest.

A line of leaf-cutter ants taking leaves back to their nests.

Butterflies cannot sting or bite their attackers like other insects. But they do have ways of keeping safe. Some species can disguise themselves. They can make themselves look like part of the bush or branch they are resting on. Others have bright colours that are meant to scare away enemies. Their colours seem to warn birds and other predators "Don't eat me. I taste awful."

SOMETHING TO DO

1. Summarize in an organizer what you have learned about plant-eating animals. Set up five columns for your organizer. In the first column write the name of the animal being recorded. Label the other columns: description of animal; habits (daytime or nocturnal); habitat (in which storey of the rainforest it lives); and diet.

2. Brainstorm a list of Canadian animals that are nocturnal.

All animals must find food in order to live. They may eat plants, fruit, insects or even other animals. Some eat only one food. Others eat many kinds of food. In Canada many people eat cows and cows eat grass. This is called a food chain.

people ⟶ cows ⟶ grass

An example of a simple Amazon food chain is: eagles eat monkeys and the monkeys eat fruit. The food chain would look like this:

eagle ⟶ monkey ⟶ fruit

PREDATORS AND PREY

At the top of the animal food chain in the rainforest are the **predators**. These animals eat other animals. Not all predators are big and fierce like the jaguar. You will be surprised to find that some birds, insects, and reptiles are predators too. We call any creature hunted or caught for food **prey**.

JAGUAR

Jaguars are big wild cats. They weigh as much as a large human being. They are well adapted for hunting in the rainforest. Their sharp claws are used to catch their prey. Strong teeth and powerful jaws allow them to tear up and eat the meat. The spotted coat of the jaguar makes it hard to see in the dim light of the understorey. Animals that are coloured to blend in with their background are wearing **camouflage**. Camouflage makes some animals hard to see and protects them from predators. In the case of the jaguar, the camouflage helps the predator get close to its prey.

Jaguars can climb into the canopy and leap from branch to branch. So monkeys and birds are not safe. The peccary or wild pig is the jaguar's favourite food, but wild pigs travel in herds of 50 or more. When attacked they charge their attacker from all sides. A herd of pigs could easily wound or kill the big cat on the ground. So the jaguar waits in a tree for the herd to pass. It drops down on a single pig, kills it, and leaps back into the tree. Crouching on a branch, the jaguar is out of the reach of the pigs. When they wander off, the jaguar comes down to eat.

The photo shows a female jaguar (left) with her partly grown cub. Jaguars are excellent swimmers.

The tamandua is a tree-dweller. It uses its thick tail to hang on to branches.

TAMANDUA (ANTEATER)

The tamandua has massive front claws and front legs that are powerful enough to tear open termite or ant nests. Once the nest is open, the tamandua uses its tongue to eat. Its tongue is lined with small, backward-pointing barbs and is coated with a sticky substance. The tongue thrashes back and forth up to 150 times each minute. Like a conveyer belt, the tongue whips termites or ants back into the tamandua's mouth. The tamandua never demolishes a whole termite nest. It always leaves enough insects to rebuild the nest. Then it can return for another meal in the future.

INSECTS

Army Ants

There are even insects that are predators. Army ants are found in huge colonies in the rain-forest. At times they go on the march. Millions of ants form columns like an army. A column is many metres in width. As the ants march forward they eat everything in their path. Lizards, snakes, insects, nesting birds and other animals are all devoured. They will even march into houses. When army ants approach their houses, the Aboriginal Peoples simply get out of the way. The ants won't harm the house but they will clear it of all mice, cockroaches, and other small animals. It is better to get out of the way of the ants' pincer jaws.

Birds too can be predators. The harpy eagle perches in the tall trees of the emergent layer. It swoops down on unsuspecting monkeys, sloths, and birds in the canopy. It is amazingly strong and agile. The harpy eagle has massive claws and a strong hooked beak. It can easily grab an adult monkey from the canopy and carry it away.

Army ants on the march. They have formed an "ant bridge" from one branch to another. The rest of the colony can pass over the bridge without losing any time.

21

The tarantula is a deadly spider.

SNAKES

Anacondas and Boa Constrictors

Anacondas and boa constrictors are two of the world's biggest snakes. Anacondas hunt along the river's edge. They prey on animals that come down to the water to drink. They will attack large and small rodents, wild pigs, deer, birds, and even crocodiles. The anaconda kills by coiling around its victim and squeezing it to death. Often the anaconda will drag its prey into the water and kill by drowning it. They do not attack humans.

Other large snakes, called boa constrictors, hunt on land. Boas lie motionless on a branch in the canopy. When a monkey or some other animal wanders into its path, it attacks. The boa strikes with its mouth open and grips with its fangs. At the same time it coils around its prey. Each time the animal breathes out the boa tightens its grip. Slowly, it squeezes its prey to death. Some Amazon tribes keep boa constrictors as pets to rid their houses of rats and mice.

The Tarantula

The tarantula is sometimes called "danger on eight legs." By day it hides in a silk-lined burrow. At night it emerges to hunt. It eats insects, small animals, and birds. It kills its prey by injecting a strong poisonous venom into it. The tarantula can give humans a very nasty bite if it is disturbed.

Anacondas have been known to grow to 10 metres in length and weigh 200 kg. Their backs are dark green with black blotches that are excellent camouflage. Their bellies are yellow with black markings. They live in the water and are excellent swimmers.

FROGS

Hundreds of different kinds of frogs live in the rainforest. Some live on the ground; others live in trees. Most frogs have the large mouth of a predator. They just sit and wait for the prey to approach. Frogs will eat insects, lizards, and even other frogs.

A gold and black poison arrow frog.
Some of the most colourful frogs in the Amazon are highly poisonous. They are visible and active all day. No animal, bird, or snake wants to come near them. If touched, these frogs ooze poison through their skin. A snake that touched a poison frog would twist and turn in pain. If the snake lived, it would never approach one of these frogs again.

SOMETHING TO DO

1. Sort out the following words and put them in the correct order of a food chain, arranging them from top to bottom.
   termites, rotting wood, anteater, jaguar

2. Try and find me! Make a picture puzzle. Draw some animals and birds in their rainforest environment. See if you can camouflage them so they are hard to spot. Colour the animals the same as they would appear in the rainforest. Then fill in the background around them. Challenge your class-mates to find and name the animals you have drawn.

3. Place pictures of rainforest animals in the correct layers on your rainforest bulletin board display.

4. Choose an animal that lives in the Amazon rainforest and find out all you can about it. How is it able to survive? Collect or draw pictures of your chosen animal. Place these in a scrapbook and include any information about the animal you were able to find.

5. Create an organizer to show what you have learned about predators. Set up five columns for your organizer. Label the columns: name; description of animal; habits; habitat (in which storey of the rainforest it lives); and diet. In the first column write the name of the animal. Write what you have learned in each column.

DID YOU KNOW?

Some Aboriginal Peoples use frogs to poison the darts for their blowguns. To collect the poison they carefully steer a frog into a cage. Then they just rub the tip of the dart on the frog's back.

nother name for rainfall or snow is **precipitation**. On this page you can see a bar graph for the average precipitation in Manaus, Brazil.

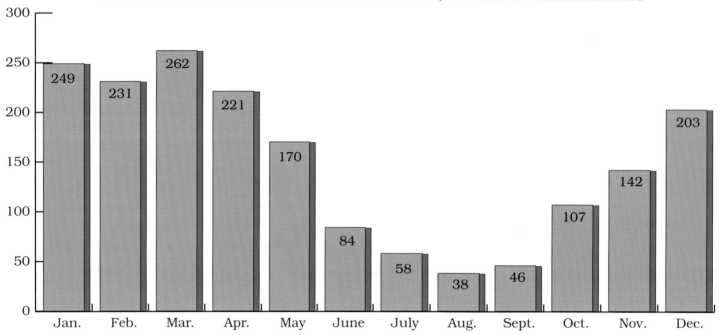

AVERAGE MONTHLY RAINFALL IN MANAUS, BRAZIL IN MILLIMETRES

HOW MUCH RAIN FALLS IN A RAINFOREST?

Read the bar graph to find out:

1. How much rain usually falls in Manaus in June?

2. In what month does the most rain fall in Manaus? In what month does the least rain fall?

3. Use your atlas or almanac to find out how these figures compare with your area.

4. Add up the monthly amounts of rainfall for Manaus for one year. Geographers use the following descriptions when talking about amounts of yearly rainfall:

- Sparse—under 250 mm per year
- Light—between 250–499 mm per year
- Moderate—between 500–999 mm per year
- Heavy—between 1000–1999 mm per year
- Very Heavy—over 2000 mm per year

What is the average yearly amount of rainfall for Manaus? Can it be considered Sparse, Light, Moderate, Heavy, or Very Heavy?

What would be the answers to the same questions for the place in Canada where you live?

HOW HOT DOES IT GET IN THE RAINFOREST?

Make a Bar Graph

Follow these steps to make a bar graph to show the average monthly temperatures in Manaus, Brazil.

1. Draw a bar graph similar to the one to the right. Mark the months along the bottom of your graph. The space between two lines stands for a month. The names of the months are part of the **legend**. The legend tells what the lines and bars mean.

2. Use the chart below the bar graph to find the average temperature for each month of the year in Manaus. The temperatures are given in degrees Celcius. Now mark the vertical line on your bar graph to show the temperature scale. Start with 0 degrees at the bottom. Number by 5 until you get to 35 at the top line. Each long line stands for 5 degrees.

3. Now put the information about the temperatures on your graph. Using the scale at the side of the graph, mark the average temperature for each month. Draw a line across each month.

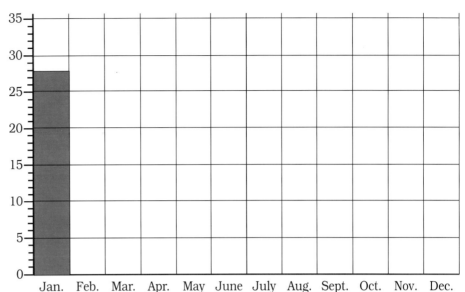

January has been done for you on the sample.

4. When you have finished, colour from the bottom line up to the lines you have drawn.

5. Give your graph a title that tells what is being compared.

Average Monthly Temperatures in Manaus, Brazil (in Celsius)	
Jan.	28°C
Feb.	28°C
Mar.	28°C
Apr.	27°C
May	28°C
June	28°C
July	28°C
Aug.	28°C
Sept.	29°C
Oct.	30°C
Nov.	29°C
Dec.	28°C

SOMETHING TO DO

1. Exchange temperature graphs with a partner. Read your partner's bar graph to find out the following:

   a) What is the highest monthly temperature in Manaus? In what month does it occur?

   b) What is the coolest month in Manaus?

2. With your partner, compare these temperatures to average monthly temperatures for the place where you live.

aria and her family are Yanomami people. The Yanomami are just one of hundreds of tribes of Aboriginal Peoples living in the Amazon. The Yanomami live in the deepest part of the rainforest near the border of Brazil and Venezuela.

*The yano is a huge dwelling in the shape of a circle. From above it would look like a giant doughnut. The wide open space in the middle is called the **plaza**. The plaza is about 30 metres across.*

A VILLAGE UNDER ONE ROOF

Maria, her brothers, sisters, and parents live in a big circular house called a **yano**. Aunts, uncles, cousins, grandparents, and other people related by marriage live there too. One Yanomami house holds about 20 families. The whole Yanomami village lives together under one roof.

Everything the Yanomami need to make their homes is found in the rainforest. The yano is made of a framework of four rings of thick poles, one inside the other. The outside ring has poles less than two meters high. Each ring gets higher as you move toward the middle. The inside ring has poles about nine metres high. The frame of the roof is made of thin poles lashed together with liana ropes. The roof and the outside wall of the yano is covered with **thatch**. Thatch is made of palm leaves, overlapped and tied together. The thatch keeps out every drop of rain. The roof overhangs the walls so that the rain just runs off the slanted roof. There is a door into the house but no windows. The plaza wall is left open.

More than 20 families, about 100 Yanomami people, live under the roof of Maria's yano. Each family has its own fire around the ring of the plaza. At their fire the family members eat, sleep, and store their belongings. It is not very private but it is their own living space. In the photo, what kind of food can you see hanging above the hammocks?

The plaza belongs to the whole village. It is a wide open space with a floor of beaten earth. Many of the activities of the community take place here. Children play in the plaza. People meet there to discuss when and where they will hunt.

The Yanomami sleep in hanging beds called hammocks. These beds swing between two poles. Hammocks are made of woven cotton or bark and knotted with cords made from vines. Everybody has a hammock except for small children who sleep with their mothers. Inside the house are everyday utensils. There are woven baskets for carrying food, eating bowls made from hollow gourds, and one or two metal pots. Bows, arrows, blowguns, spears, and other weapons are kept inside the yano. These few possessions are stored on shelves or hung on the walls of the house. But there is no other furniture in the house.

The family fire burns day and night. It is used for cooking and to keep the mosquitoes away. The fire gives warmth in the cool, damp rainforest nights. During the night, each member of the family must take turns getting up to tend the fire.

SOMETHING TO DO

1. List the materials the Yanomami use to construct their homes.

   a) Where do they get the materials?

   b) How do they use the materials to protect their homes against the weather?

   c) How are their homes suited to their way of life?

2. Make a model of a yano. Roll out plasticine in a big sheet. Collect sticks or twigs of various lengths. Make four rings of twigs. The inner ring is the highest. The outer ring is the lowest. Place the sticks as upright posts in the plasticine. Make a framework of thin twigs for the roof. Tie the twigs to the upright posts. Thatch the roof with dried grass, leaves, or strips of paper. Set your yano on a large piece of bristol board. Colour in the rainforest, the gardens, and the river. (For more information on gardens and rivers, see Chapters 12 and 13.)

E veryone in Maria's family has a job to do. They either hunt or they gather and prepare food. Maria's father and older brothers hunt to supply the family with meat and fish. Every day they set off early into the rainforest. They may hunt alone or in groups of two or three. They are gone for most of the day. They may walk 15 or 20 kilometres before returning.

The Yanomami hunt with bows, rifles, and blowguns. They prefer the bow and the blowgun because these weapons are silent. The noise of rifle fire frightens the animals away.

Yanomami hunters kill only enough to feed the tribe. They know that if they catch too many birds, animals, and fish there will be fewer to feed their children in the future.

Maria's father made a blowgun more than two metres long from the hollow stem of the bamboo plant. With it he hunts monkeys and birds high up in the canopy. He places a poisoned dart in one end of the pipe. The point of the dart has been tipped with a coating of **curare**. Curare is a powerful poison made from the bark or roots of some Strychnos vines. He blows air through the stem. Only a puff of air is needed to blow the dart about 10 metres. A wounded monkey could escape into the tangle of trees and vines, but curare from the dart affects the lungs of the animal. Soon it cannot breathe and falls to the ground. Maria's father seldom misses.

Wild honey is one of the favourite foods of the Yanomami. Sometimes a hunter will spot a bee-hive high up inside hollow branches of a tree. The hunter shins up the tree and chops off the branch. The branch crashes to the ground and he quickly slides down the tree. With his axe he cuts into the branch. He pulls out the honeycombs and stands licking his fingers. Angry bees buzzing around don't seem to bother him. Then he wraps the honey in a palm leaf and carries it back to the yano.

Yanomami hunters are very generous with what they catch. They share everything they catch with everyone else. If a man is too ill or old to hunt, his family receive a share anyway. A hunter does not eat any of what he kills. It is given to others. Yanomami hunters believe that the spirit of the hawk guides them in the hunt. They are afraid that the hawk spirit will not help anyone who eats what he has killed. A hunter will only eat what another hunter shares with him.

Yanomami hunters use arrows that are taller than they are. Their arrows are made from the cane of a plant that grows in the forest. Arrowheads are fashioned from sharpened strips of bamboo, monkey bone, or thin points of palm wood. The bows are about two metres long. They are strung with fibre from a plant the Yanomami grow in their gardens.

DID YOU KNOW?

Curare is used in modern surgery to relax patients during operations. This drug was not discovered in a laboratory, but by rainforest people.

This photograph shows a Yanomami boy with bow and arrow. Boys also catch fish using the poisonous vines of a certain tree. They drag the vines through shallow parts of the river. Poison sap from the vines pollutes the water temporarily. The fish become drugged and begin to die. Then the boys scoop up the fish in nets. Eating the poisoned fish does not harm the Yanomami people.

SOMETHING TO DO

1. How do the Yanomami use the resources of their natural environment to obtain food?

2. South American hunters tie their poison-tipped arrows together with cord. They keep them securely in a quiver. Why do you think they do this?

3. Would you like to live in the Amazon rainforest? Write down the reasons for your answer.

4. Think, pair, square. Think about the following question and write down your thoughts.

   Why do you think a Yanomami hunter could probably obtain all the food needed with a bow and arrow, yet a person from somewhere else in the world would probably starve in the rainforest?

   Next, share your ideas with a partner. Finally, you and your partner meet with another pair and share all of your best ideas.

The Yanomami grow crops in small clearings in the rainforest. They look for a spot with fertile soil near the yano. It must not be in a place where the river will flood over it. Then the men and boys cut down and burn small parts of the forest. This is called **slash and burn farming**.

Two Yanomami men in their farm clearing in the middle of the rainforest. The man in front is using a chopping tool called a machete. The plants with long green leaves are banana plants.

First the smaller trees are chopped down using axes and heavy knives. The branches are piled around the bottom of the larger trees. When the wood has dried they set it on fire. Some larger trees may not burn completely. However, enough space has been cleared to plant crops. The fire destroys weed seeds and insects. The ashes contain minerals that actually make the soil richer.

When the garden has been cleared, the Yanomami people get ready to plant their crops. The men make holes in the soft earth with a digging stick. Then women and girls plant the seeds.

Favourite crops are manioc, maize, yams, and **plantain**. Plantains are like large bananas. Maria and the women plant canes that will be used for making arrows and cotton for making hammocks. Pineapples, papaya, bananas, and palm trees are also placed in the gardens. The trees will take 3 to 10 years to produce fruit. But families will return to pick the fruit long after the village has moved to a new place.

Crops grow quickly in the warm moist ground but only enough is harvested for each meal. It is impossible to store food for more than a few days in this hot, wet climate.

It may surprise you that the soil in the Amazon is not very **fertile** or good for growing crops. The forest must rely on its own dead leaves and rain for nourishment. After three years, rain washes away most of the minerals from the garden's soil. Crops no longer grow well. Then the whole Yanomami village must move on. They build a new yano, clear new gardens and start over. This kind of farming is called **shifting cultivation**. Shifting cultivation does not harm the forest because the gardens are small. The rainforest quickly grows back and no lasting damage has been done.

FOOD FOR THE YANOMAMI

Maria and her mother and sisters plant and look after the small gardens. They also collect nuts and wild fruit. There are over 200 species of fruit in the forest to choose from. Women cook for the family, look after the children, gather firewood and keep the yano tidy. They also weave hammocks and loincloths.

Maria's family loves to eat meat. Monkey, deer, wild pig, toucans, and anteater are favourites. Certain snakes are also enjoyed as food. People who have tried it say that snake meat tastes like chicken. Crocodile eggs, turtles, frogs, land crabs, and roasted termites are special treats.

The Yanomami make soup from plantains. They also make a sweet drink by mixing honey and water.

Manioc is the food eaten at every meal. It is as important to the Yanomami as bread is to Canadians. Manioc is a fast-growing plant but only its roots are eaten. Strangely, manioc roots are poisonous but the Yanomami know how to get rid of the poison.

First Maria and her mother grate manioc roots on a board studded with sharp fish teeth. Then they soak the manioc in water and squeeze it to remove the poison juices. This process is repeated over and over. Next the manioc is left to dry in the hot sun. Now it is ready to be ground into flour and baked into round flat cakes. Pieces of cooked fish are sometimes rolled up in these cakes.

SOMETHING TO DO

1. What foods do the Yanomami eat? Describe how some of the foods were prepared. Include sketches.

2. The Yanomami are farmers. What advantages does farming give them? What problems or difficulties do they face as farmers?

3. The Yanomami practice good conservation of their environment. In small groups discuss how they use the rainforest without causing long-term damage.

DID YOU KNOW?

Canadians also eat manioc. We call it tapioca and usually serve it in the form of a pudding.

*J*ust before dawn, the Yanomami slip out of their hammocks and hurry to the river to take a bath. The water of the river is much warmer and more comfortable than the chilly early morning air. It is like taking a warm bath. It is the first of several dips they will take during the day.

About noon people take another swim in the river. This time they use the water of the river to cool off. Again, in the mid-afternoon most return to splash about in the water. By afternoon the heat of the rainforest is almost unbearable. No wonder few clothes are needed or worn in the hot rainforest.

BODY DECORATION

The Yanomami do not wear many clothes because of the heat. Instead they prefer to decorate their bodies with paint. Both women and men paint and decorate their bodies. Red body paint is worn daily. On special occasions they add black paint as well. For feasts, they love to get really dressed up. They wear body paint and colourful jewellery made from feathers and beads.

All the ornaments come from nature. Flowers and leaves are picked in the rainforest. They are worn in pierced ears much as we would wear earrings. Brightly coloured parrot or toucan feathers are tucked into armbands. Sometimes soft bird down is stuck on the head. Women wear twigs and reeds stuck through holes in their nose and lower lip. Both men and women wear strings of beads made of shells or nuts.

Patterns are painted on bodies and faces using dyes made from plants. The vivid red dye comes from a plant called **urucu** which the Yanomami grow in their gardens. It is smeared right on to the body, or it is made into a paste and painted on with a stick. For a

This Yanomami man has painted his face red then decorated it with black dots. He is ready for a feast.

Everyday Life among the Yanomami

A young girl has pierced her nose and face with pieces of straw. What other decorations is she wearing?

contrast colour, the Yanomami use black. The black comes from charcoal or the fruit of the **genipapo** tree. Black is supposed to suggest courage.

Putting on paint is a group activity. Mothers and fathers decorate their children. Wives make up their husbands. Girls take turns painting each other. The painter and the wearer choose the designs. Animal markings are popular. Splotchy spots suggest the jaguar, which is a much admired beast. Another favourite design is to paint with wavy lines. Another is to cover all parts of the body black, except the face, hands and feet. Then the person looks like the quick-moving black spider monkey. See the photo on page 36 that shows a man painted in this dramatic style.

Two Yanomami girls decorate each other before a feast. The girl on the right has been painted with jaguar "spots."

SOMETHING TO DO

1. Imagine you could interview a Yanomami girl or boy about your own age. What questions would you ask about body painting? Stage the interview with a partner.

2. Suggest reasons why the Yanomami would want to paint themselves as a jaguar or monkey.

Yanomami children spend the first three years of life close to their mothers. From age three to 13, boys play in groups. They roam through the yano, running wildly and playing rough, noisy games. They seldom return to their family, except to eat and sleep. They spend the whole day running with their friends.

The games the boys play prepare them for adult life. They climb trees to the topmost branches. They hunt with miniature bows and arrows which they have made. No small animal, toad, or lizard is safe from their attack. Here a boy chases his pet bird across the unfinished roof of a yano.

There is no formal teaching but there is a lot to learn. Boys learn by watching and imitating others. A boy must know how to make weapons, to recognize animal tracks, and to hunt. He must also learn how to clear the forest for a garden, to build a yano, and to defend the village.

From 14 years onwards boys are treated as adults. They start to hunt seriously now and use full-size weapons. By 14 they are expected to help provide food for the yano.

Yanomami girls also play in groups with other girls and sometimes with the boys. But girls spend more time with adults than boys do. Their life is not as carefree. Girls help older women with the babies, fetch water, or go on expeditions to collect food in the forest. There is a lot for a girl to learn. She has to know how to plant crops and grow gardens. She must

know what wood makes good firewood and how to prepare food and cook it. She must be able to look after a family. She must also be able to spin cotton and weave hammocks.

Girls like Maria marry at about age 15. Boys marry later, in their twenties. Young men have to earn the right to marry. For several years they must work for their future parents-in-law. They must supply their intended wife and her family with meat they have killed. Before they can marry they must prove that they are good hunters and providers. Young men show their hunting skill by wearing the most beautiful feathers of the birds they have shot.

Vine baskets decorated with dye from the urucu plant.

ARTS AND CRAFTS

Part of growing up for the Yanomami means learning certain crafts. The Yanomami have few possessions. Everything is made for a practical purpose. The things they make will be used in daily life.

It might be baskets for carrying food. It might be sharp-tipped arrows to use in the hunt. It could be something that will be worn at a ceremony or feast. Ceremonial objects are usually created out of materials such as feathers, flowers, and leaves. Each adult person makes his or her own decorations. They are all beautiful and made with great care.

There are no special craft makers in the tribe. The only specialization is between men and women. Women do certain crafts, so girls learn to do these things. Men do other crafts. All men make their own weapons and share in building the yano, so boys learn to do these crafts.

The Yanomami also grow cotton in their garden plots. Women in the tribe use the cotton to weave hammocks and nets and to make different pieces of clothing.

Yanomami boys putting feathers on their arrows.

All women make woven cane baskets, back-packs woven from palm leaves, and hammocks for sleeping.

SOMETHING TO DO

1. Even though Yanomami children don't go to school, what important lessons do they learn? Do you think Yanomami children are well prepared to be adults? Why?

2. In groups, discuss how Yanomami children learn. Compare the way they are educated with the way you are educated today. How are the methods different? How are they similar? Which method of educating children do you prefer? Why?

3. Write a short story to describe what parts of growing up among the Yanomami you would enjoy most. Be sure you tell your reader why you think the way you do.

The Yanomami love giving parties. They choose times of the year when food is plentiful and travel is easy. The feast could mark an important event such as a marriage or a death. It could celebrate a good harvest. Someone is sent from the yano with invitations for neighbours. These neighbours may live a two or three day walk away through the forest.

One of the guests does the Presentation Dance. He is painted black to look like a spider monkey. His hair is decorated with bird down.

The village starts collecting huge amounts of food for the party. They cook vast quantities of soup made from plantains. Wild meat is hunted and then smoked over fires. Manioc roots are ground and stacks of manioc bread are baked.

Finally the day of the party arrives. A shout goes up that the guests have been spotted coming down a trail through the rainforest. All the people of the yano quickly paint and decorate their bodies. They want to be wearing their finest decorations when the visitors arrive.

The first visitor appears in the yano. He runs into the plaza and lets out a whoop. He comes ahead of the others to announce that they are approaching. This visitor is beautifully painted with urucu. Two bright blue feathers of the rare hyacinth macaw are worn in his ears.

The head man of the yano welcomes the first visitor with a formal speech. Then the other visitors arrive. The men run wildly into the yano. First, they circle around the ring of the plaza and then gather in the centre. The guests begin to stamp their feet and chant faster and faster until the pace becomes quite frenzied. Suddenly they stop. This is called the Presentation Dance. It is the way visitors introduce themselves at a feast. Then the women guests, who were waiting at the entrance, come into the yano.

Now it is the turn of the men of the host yano to show how brave they are. They rush around the plaza banging their spears and looking ferocious. They are showing that they are brave hunters who could defend their village. It is as if they are warning their guests—"Don't get any ideas of attacking us while you are enjoying the feast!"

When they are full, the Yanomami and their guests start to dance. Women dance with women. Men dance with men. They dance in a line with their arms around each other's backs or shoulders. Dancers move in quick short steps, almost like walking. The steps follow a repeated pattern—four steps forward, three steps back. They chant or sing as they dance. The chanting and dancing continue long into the night.

The feast may last for three or more days. During that time

legends and stories are told and vast amounts of food are eaten. Before the guests leave, more food is prepared. It is laid out on palm leaves in the plaza. There are huge piles of boiled meat and manioc bread. This food is packed into baskets and given to each of the visiting families as they leave.

The women guests leave the yano first. One by one, the men follow them. They go in typical Yanomami fashion. They make no gesture of farewell. They do not say "thank you for the nice party" or even "good-bye." All they say as they leave is "I am going home."

The soup party is over.

The guests are shown to a fireplace where a long, hollowed-out log is filled with plantain soup. They are served soup in bowls made of gourds. The soup party begins. Everyone is urged to eat bowl after bowl until they can eat no more.

SOMETHING TO DO

1. Work in groups to plan and hold a Yanomami feast. Divide into guests and hosts or invite another class. Plan the event carefully. Send out invitations to the guests. Prepare food. Write down some legends that can be told at the feast. Practice a Presentation Dance. Decorate your faces with body paint and colourful costumes. Have a soup party.

When their guests arrive, the men of the host yano gather in a large group. They all shout and shake their spears. They are ready to defend their yano in case of attack.

The Yanomami believe in a world of spirits. They believe every person, animal, bird, fish, and plant has an invisible spirit. Sometimes these spirits leave their bodies and wander around the forest. Such spirits can cause trouble. The spirits of animals can be angry if the Yanomami have been greedy and killed too many. The Yanomami believe that spirits of enemy tribes can come from far away to hurt them. They do this by blowing an invisible poison dart into a person's body. Instantly that person falls ill or some misfortune strikes him or his family.

To help them face the world of spirits the Yanomami turn to the **shaman**, a person who knows about spirits. He has the ability to call on his own spirits to help. Shamans take drugs made from plants of the rainforest to help them see the invisible spirits.

The Yanomami believe the shaman is powerful in other ways too. His powers over spirits can bring good luck in hunting. Sometimes the shaman can prevent bad storms and drive away spirits sent by enemy tribes to hurt the yano.

LEGENDS

The Yanomami love to tell stories called **legends** at their feasts. Legends have been passed down from parents to children for hundreds of years. They are not written down but are told over and over again around the campfire. Legends answer questions people ask. How was the world created? Why are the animals as they are? Why is the environment the way it is? Who are the great hunters and leaders of our people?

Here is a Yanomami legend from the Amazon rainforest.

The Yanomami who are sick turn to the shaman for help. He gives them remedies made from roots and plants. He also tries to draw out the invisible poison dart that the bad spirit has blown into the sick person's body. The boy in the photo is suffering from malaria, a tropical disease.

How the Yanomami Stole the Jaguar's Fire

A boy and his sister's husband went to a cliff where macaws were nesting. They found a pole and the boy climbed up to look in the nest.

When the boy looked in the nest he saw birds. Instead of throwing them down to his brother-in-law, he threw a stone. The stone hit the brother-in-law's hand. It made him angry. He knocked away the pole and went home. The boy was left stranded on the cliff.

Night fell and no one came. The next day he began to be thirsty. Three days passed. Then the boy heard the roar of a jaguar. The boy called down to the jaguar. He offered to throw the jaguar a young macaw if he would rescue him.

The boy threw one macaw down and the jaguar ate it. He threw down another and another. When the jaguar had eaten all the macaws he got the pole and set it against the cliff. The boy scrambled down.

This jaguar was friendly and took the boy to his own house. At the jaguar's house there was a fire with meat being cooked over it. The jaguar gave him the first cooked meat the boy had ever eaten. It was delicious. The boy's own people did not have fire at that time. The boy decided to remain with the jaguar.

But the jaguar's wife did not like the boy. One day, when the jaguar was out, she threatened him. The boy was terrified. He took his bow and arrow and shot the jaguar's wife. Then he was afraid of what the jaguar would do when he came home. So the boy ran back to his own village.

He told his family about the fire and how delicious cooked meat was. They went back to the jaguar's house. While the jaguar slept, the people stole his fire. The jaguar woke up cold and his house was dark. He was very angry. Now the people had fire and the jaguar had none.

The jaguar roared angrily at the people for stealing his fire. The jaguar said, "If that is how you act, from now on I'm going to eat you!"

That is why jaguars are so full of hatred for people and attack them in the forest.

The jaguar helped the Yanomami boy climb down from the high cliff.

The jaguar was furious that the Yanomami had stolen his fire.

SOMETHING TO DO

1. What powers do the Yanomami believe the shaman has?

2. In small groups, discuss and list the answers to these questions.

   • What questions does this legend about the jaguar's fire answer?

   • What values or customs of the people does the legend explain?

3. Try writing a legend to explain what causes thunderstorms or why the people eat manioc.

The first Europeans to live in the Amazon were Portuguese. Some Portuguese settlers married Aboriginal women. Their descendants are a mixed-race people. They call themselves **caboclos**.

The caboclos live along the river and depend on it for their simple way of life. The river provides fish to eat and water for drinking and washing. Their small huts are built on stilts on the muddy riverbanks. During the flood season, the stilt houses have water up to their floor level.

THE CABOCLOS

Most caboclos are very poor. They use lines, nets, and spears to catch fish for food and to sell in the market at Manaus. Their food is mainly manioc flour mixed with fish. Most grow fruit and vegetables in small gardens and keep a few chickens. Some caboclos earn a living as rubber tappers. Others grow a crop called **jute** in the flood plains near the river. The fibre of the jute plant is used to make burlap sacks and backing for carpets. Some caboclos hire themselves out to work on one of the large cattle ranches. Here they help with the cattle or clear and burn land for new fields.

For the caboclos the nearest hospital is usually hours away by boat. Getting sick in the rainforest is a serious problem. Government schools are badly equipped with few books or supplies. Teachers are not well trained and children aren't taught much more than a little reading and addition and subtraction. Parents cannot afford to send their children to better schools in town or pay for them to learn a trade. So few children of the caboclos ever get steady jobs.

RANCHERS

Few people went to the Amazon rainforest until 1975, when the Trans-Amazonian Highway was opened. It was the first of a number of large roads that cut through the rainforest. The Brazilian government built these roads hoping that millions of poor people from the coastal cities of Brazil would move to the Amazon and become farmers and ranchers.

New roads brought thousands into the rainforest. Using chainsaws, they cut down trees and set them on fire. They tried to plant cash crops such as coffee. They also cleared fields for their cattle to graze. However, rainforest soil does not produce very nutritious grass for cattle to eat. In order to get enough to eat, one beef cow must have a large area to graze on. This means more and more trees and plants have to be destroyed.

Most of the cattle raised here are only good for pet food and soups. When the land is worn out, the ranchers move on and slash and burn another area. They leave behind vast empty stretches of forest that will never recover.

MINERS

Roads also brought in mining companies and individual prospectors looking for gold in the tributaries of the Amazon. Miners live in the forest in huge towns that are as lawless as the towns of the old Wild West.

The gold miners do not dig deep shafts into the earth. Instead, they look for gold in open pit mines and river beds. Their excavations of river valleys destroy the fish on which the Aboriginal Peoples depend. Large mining operations pollute the rivers with toxic mercury. They also pollute the air by burning tremendous amounts of wood from the forest.

In 1989, 40 000 gold miners arrived in the territory of the Yanomami. Up to this time the Yanomami had had very little contact with the outside world. The miners brought diseases with them that the Yanomami had never had before, such as colds, flu, and measles. The Yanomami got very sick because they had no resistance to these germs. By 1990, 15 percent of the Yanomami had died of measles, flu, and common colds.

SOMETHING TO DO

1. Think, pair, square. In what ways have roads been a good and bad thing for the Amazon rainforests? Write down as many ideas as you can. Then share your ideas with a partner. Listen to your partner's ideas. Make a joint list. Rank all the ideas from most important to least important. Then meet with another pair and compare your lists.

2. The Yanomami practiced "slash and burn" and "shifting cultivation." The rainforest always recovered quickly. In what way is the clearing of rainforest for ranching and farming different?

3. One of the biggest dangers to the Yanomami is disease. Thousands of forest people have died because they caught diseases such as colds, flu, and measles. Why are these diseases so serious to forest people when they often cause only mild illness for us?

here are only a few big towns in the Amazon region. Two of the biggest are Belem and Manaus.

The Amazon port city of Belem.

Belem lies near the mouth of the Amazon, about 120 km from the Atlantic Ocean. It was founded in the sixteenth century by the Portuguese. Today, more than a million people live in Belem. It is a major river and ocean port.

About 1600 km further inland is the city of Manaus. Manaus developed on the site of an old Portuguese fort. It is on the north shore of the Rio Negro, about 18 km upstream from where this tributary joins the Amazon River.

Manaus is the major industrial and commercial centre of the Amazon. More than a million people live there. Most of them are descendants of Europeans and Africans. They are the grandchildren of early settlers from Portugal, Spain, and Africa. Portuguese is the main language spoken.

The government of Brazil has encouraged business and industry to move to Manaus by making it a tax-free city. For example, Japanese electronics companies have moved there. They employ local people to assemble computers, televisions, and motor-bikes. The city is a mixture of modern buildings, stores, fine homes, and offices. But alongside these are terrible slums. Poor people live in thatched shacks on stilts along the river.

In the early days, Manaus was the wealthiest city in South America. People who lived there made huge fortunes in the rubber business. Many beautiful public buildings and homes were built at that time. Life was very comfortable in Manaus even in the middle of the rain-forest. Manaus had electric street lights before London, England. It had electric street cars before many cities in Europe and the United States. The great wealth of Manaus ended about 1915, when cheaper rubber began to be produced in Asian plantations.

City dwellers of Manaus and Belem rise by 5 or 6 a.m. Breakfast is bread and a cup of Brazilian coffee with hot milk and plenty of sugar. By 7 o'clock the people are off to work in offices, factories, markets, wharves, and stores. They prefer to work during the morning before it gets very hot.

Instead of taking an hour for lunch, people take three hours for lunch and a siesta. A siesta is a short period of rest during the day.

After a big lunch, it is time for a nap. When siesta is over, people return to work. They make up the hours of the siesta by working later in the cooler afternoon and evening hours until about 7 o'clock. You might think that the siesta means that people are lazy. You would be wrong. The siesta means that townspeople of the Amazon have learned how to live in a very hot climate.

Dinner doesn't start until 9 or 10 o'clock at night. A favourite meal is a fish stew called **peixada** prepared from one of the excellent fish caught in the Amazon River. Fish is eaten daily because it is so plentiful. After dinner the family often goes for a late night walk to enjoy the cooler evening temperatures.

Theatro Amazonas, the grand opera house of Manaus is an example of the great wealth of Manaus when it was first founded.

SOMETHING TO DO

1. To compare life in three places make a three-column organizer with these three headings:

LIFE IN MY AREA OF CANADA	LIFE IN MANAUS AND BELEM	LIFE AMONG THE YANOMAMI

Place the phrases from the list below in the columns each describes. Some phrases may appear in only one column. Some phrases will be repeated in more than one column. If you can't find the details in the book make guesses from what you know.

- People plant crops for food.
- Homes contain modern appliances.
- People wear little clothing.
- People go hunting for their food.
- People buy most goods from markets and stores.
- People regularly take a siesta.
- People use many different tools and equipment.
- People work in offices, stores, factories and schools.

- Homes are made with materials close at hand.
- People practice slash and burn farming.
- People use cars, buses, and planes to travel.
- People use scientific methods to cure sickness.
- People go to school.
- People live close to all their relatives.
- People live with their immediate family only.

2. What did you observe from your organizer? What features do people living in these three areas share? Suggest reasons why this is so.

Part of the market area of Manaus. Why do you think each market stall has a covering of some sort?

uropeans had never seen rubber until they arrived in South America. Then they saw the Aboriginal Peoples bouncing rubber balls. The rubber came from trees that grew wild only in the Amazon rainforest. Rubber is made from **latex**. Latex is the milky white sap found just beneath the bark of rubber tree.

The tapper makes sloping cuts with a curved sharp knife in the bark of rubber trees. At the bottom of the cut the tapper hangs a cup. Latex drips very slowly from the cut into the cup. Every three days the latex is collected from the trees. Tappers carry their pails of latex to a central hut.

The first rubber the Europeans tried to make was not too useful. It was too gooey when hot and too stiff when cold. Then **vulcanization** was invented. Vulcanization is a process that makes rubber flexible whether it is hot or cold. Now they could make lots of useful goods from rubber. They made tires, raincoats, rubber boots, bicycle wheels, and a wide variety of other products. Manufacturing rubber became a very important business. Raw rubber was collected in the rainforest and was sent to factories all over the world. The people of Manaus got very rich on money made from the rubber business.

Then, in the late 1800s disaster struck. New and better ways were found to raise rubber trees in other parts of the world. In the Amazon forest wild rubber trees were widely scattered. Because the trees were hard to find, it was expensive to collect the latex. So, seeds from rubber trees in the Amazon were sent to England. Little trees were grown from these seeds and sent to other countries with tropical rainforests. The trees were planted on huge farms or **plantations** in Indonesia, Malaysia, Thailand, and Sri Lanka. Rubber trees growing on plantations are much easier to get at than wild trees in the forest. By 1915 many other countries were producing rubber. The prosperous days for the Amazon rubber business were over.

Today, rubber is still a major industry of the Amazon rainforest. However, Brazil produces only a small percent of the world's rubber crop.

RUBBER TAPPERS

The person who collects the latex is called a **tapper**. About 100 000 tappers live and work in the Amazon rainforest. Most tappers are caboclos.

When the tapper has a canoe-load of rubber, he brings it out of the forest to market in Manaus. At the factory in

The latex is processed into a huge ball of raw rubber. It is poured slowly onto a pole in the smoke over a fire. The tapper rotates the stick as he pours the latex. Gradually the latex thickens and sticks to the pole. This process is called curing the rubber. When he has a huge ball of thickened rubber, he cuts it off the stick. The ball of rubber, called a **bolos**, weighs about 40 kg.

Manaus, acid is added to the latex to separate the solid rubber from the liquid part. The rubber is rolled into flat sheets. When the sheets are dry they are baled up and sent to all parts of the world to be made into rubber goods.

Tappers earn their living from the forest. They are leaders in the fight to keep the rainforest from being cleared for cattle ranches and the timber business.

SOMETHING TO DO

1. To the right is a sketch of an imaginary rubber tree. Make a similar sketch in your notebook.

   a) Add to the drawing the gash the tapper makes in the bark of the rubber tree and label it.
   b) Add to the drawing the latex dripping out of the gash into the cup and label it.
   c) Name the next five steps in the making of rubber.
   d) On the branches and trunk of the tree are some uses of rubber. Think of examples of each of these and print them on the branches of the tree you have drawn.

2. Pick a dandelion leaf or flower. Notice that a white, milky liquid comes from the stem. This is a kind of latex and is similar to the latex from rubber trees. During the Second World War the Russians made rubber tires from dandelion latex. Find out what other plants produce latex.

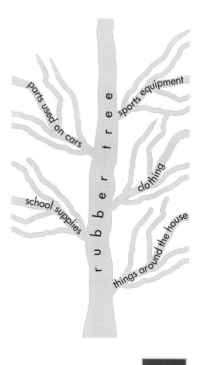

parts used on cars • sports equipment • clothing • school supplies • things around the house • rubber tree

*T*ropical rainforests have many different kinds of high-quality wood that loggers seek. Mahogany, rosewood, and teak all grow in the rainforest. These woods are very hard and resist decay. They are also beautiful to look at, and carpenters like to use them to fashion high-quality furniture. The rainforest also produces many kinds of fruit and nuts.

Brazil nuts.

BRAZIL NUTS

Brazil nuts are enjoyed around the world but most people don't know how they grow on trees. They grow like segments of an orange. Twelve to twenty-four nuts are arranged in a large wooden cup. Brazil nut trees grow 30 m high in the forest. One tree can produce 500 kg of nuts each harvest.

Since Brazil nuts ripen during the rainy season, workers have to camp in the forest in heavy rains. The trees are too tall to climb so they wait until the cup falls to the ground. However, the cups are very heavy—about the size and weight of a small cabbage. Workers are often injured when the falling wooden cups hit them on the head.

Workers gather the cups and chop off the top third with machetes. They shake out the nuts, which are then dried and shipped to market.

The Amazon rainforest produces about 50 000 metric tonnes of Brazil nuts each year. The nuts are so rich in oil that the rainforest peoples press them to get their cooking oil. They also use the empty cups as bowls and storage containers.

CACAO TREES

Did you know that one of your favourite foods comes from the cacao tree? Chocolate! Cacao trees grow wild in the Amazon rainforest.

Cacao beans have to be scooped out of the seed pods and left in the hot sun for two or three weeks. Then the beans are poured into sacks and shipped to Europe, the United States, and other parts of the world.

Countries that buy the beans make them into cocoa powder and chocolate. First the beans are roasted and ground into cocoa powder. Then the workers make chocolate by mixing cocoa, sugar, and milk. They

THE PRODUCTS OF RAINFOREST TREES

Rainforest Tree	Products
rubber	latex sap is used to make rubber for raincoats, boots, shoe soles, tires, balls, and many other things
mahogany	a hard wood used for expensive furniture
balsa	a light wood used for wooden parts in airplanes
banana	produces fruit
brazil and cashew	produce nuts
carnauba palm	the wax from its leaves is used in lipstick and shoe polish
sapodilla	its sap, called chicle, is used for making chewing gum
cacao	its beans are used to make chocolate

heat the mixture for three days. Then the liquid chocolate is poured into moulds to cool and harden into delicious bars of chocolate.

PINEAPPLES

The pineapple originated in the rainforests of South America, but it is now grown on plantations in many tropical countries. It is a member of the bromeliad family. Pineapple is tasty either fresh or tinned. The fibre in the leaves of the pineapple plant can also be used. It can be extracted, prepared, spun and woven to make a sheer, fine cloth.

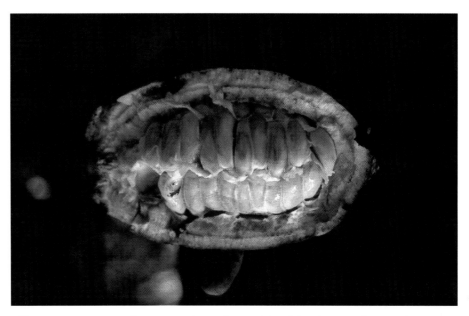

Cacao trees produce seed pods and inside the pods are beans. Beans taken right from the pod taste bitter and not at all like chocolate.

SOMETHING TO DO

1. You can grow a pineapple as a pot plant.

   - Choose a fresh, slightly green pineapple.
   - Slice off the top with about a centimetre of fruit left on it. Let it dry overnight.
   - If possible sprinkle hormone rooting powder on the base of the pineapple top.
   - Put pebbles in the bottom of the pot. Then fill it with moist compost. Place the pineapple top in the pot.
   - Cover the pineapple and pot with a plastic bag and place it in a warm, sunny window.
   - Take the bag off when new shoots appear in the centre of the pineapple top.

2. As a group project, perform a taste test of tropical fruits. Get two or three tropical fruits such as mangoes, pineapples, bananas, papayas, star fruit. If possible get fruit you have never tried before.

   - Prepare a chart for your taste test. Choose the categories you will evaluate: sweetness, texture, fragrance, attractiveness, and overall tastiness are some possibilities.
   - Peel and cut the fruit into small pieces just before the test. Place the pieces on separate plates and label them. Taste each type of fruit and rate it from 1 to 10 in each category, 10 being the highest score and 1 the lowest.
   - Add up the scores. Which fruit had the highest taste rating? Compare your findings with those of your classmates.

ou can fly into Manaus and Belem. You could travel by car or bus from Belem to Manaus. This would take several days because the distance is great and the highway is rough. There are few trains except for commuter trains in the cities. The Amazon River and its tributaries are still the most important highways for carrying people and goods.

The caboclos and Aboriginal Peoples use dug-out canoes. They are made by hollowing out a single tree trunk. Someone has said that a dug-out canoe looks like a hollow cigar. The wealthier caboclos power their canoes with outboard motors.

Commercial fishing boats bring crates of fresh fish to market. Around Manaus, motor launches make regular trips up and down the river. They stop at small villages and form a regular water-bus system. They transport people, produce, animals,

Riverboats take tourists on sight-seeing trips.

A tugboat pushes a raft of logs downstream to a sawmill. There the logs will be sawn into boards.

Transportation in the Amazon

Ocean-going ships are able to travel up the Amazon because the river is very deep. Large ships can travel as far upstream as Manaus without any trouble. Ships bring in most supplies to river ports and carry away rainforest products to the farthest corners of the world.

and almost anything that will fit on a launch. In Belem, many children go to school on a boat instead of a bus.

More and more roads are being built through the rainforest. However, even the 5000-kilometre Trans-Amazonian Highway is blocked at times. Heavy rains often wash away parts of the road. Many of the other roads are just dirt tracks. There are no bridges across the Amazon River. All trucks and cars have to be ferried across. But the government believes

that roads are needed to encourage industry to move into the Amazon rainforest. With roads you can have trucks, and when the roads are in good shape it is much faster to transport goods by truck than by riverboat.

Air traffic is also opening up the Amazon basin. Small airports have been built deep in the rainforest. This is how mining companies get workers to their isolated mines. But the rivers remain the most important way of transporting people and goods.

SOMETHING TO DO

1. If you were travelling on a boat bus from Belem to the mouth of the Amazon, in what direction would you be going? (Check the map on page 5.)

2. Brainstorm a list of supplies that might have to be brought in to Manaus from other parts of the world.

3. Draw pictures to compare the types of transportation used in your community and in the Amazon to transport people and goods. What types are similar? What types are different? How are the types of transportation changing in your own community and in the Amazon rainforest?

ould you like to visit the Amazon? Many people dream of exploring the rainforest. The chance to see nature "up close" really excites them. Seeing rainforest animals, birds, and plants in their natural habitat could be the adventure of a life-time.

Nature tourism is gaining popularity in the Amazon. This kind of tourism conserves the beauty of the rainforest. Since it is the animals, birds, and plant life of the forest that tourists pay to see, nature tourism gives businesses a reason to protect the environment.

FOREST LODGES

There are a several forest lodges around Manaus. One is called the Ariau Jungle Tower. It is built to minimize disturbance to the environment. The lodge consists of three wooden towers fit between the treetops. The towers are connected by a network of stairs and wooden walkways. The walkways are at various levels above the ground. Sleeping rooms in the hotel have thatched roofs. Guests sleep in a hammock, Amazon style.

The Ariau Jungle Tower is a hotel in the treetops. Here the visitor can walk through different layers of the rainforest. There is even a high observation tower in the emergent layer. From the tower the visitor can look down on the canopy and take photographs.

At forest lodges the tourist can expect close encounters with wild animals. Since the owners feed wild animals regularly, up to a dozen species visit the lodges. Some are so tame they will feed out of your hand. A coatimundi, a type of raccoon, may gnaw at an unattended camera. A monkey might welcome you by wrapping his tail around your neck. Squirrel monkeys, red howlers, brown capuchins and black spider monkeys swarm in the treetops. Jaguars are secretive and few visitors ever spot one.

Birdwatching from the towers is excellent. At sunrise visitors see flocks of parrots leaving their roosts for their feeding grounds. Hummingbirds feed at flowering bushes. Dozens of other species of birds can swoop by.

At night, with a flashlight, the visitor might spot red, green, or pink reflecting points in the darkness. These could be the eyes of a crocodile, frog, or a spectacled owl.

EXCURSION BOATS

Another way to explore the Amazon is to observe nature from the comfort of an excursion boat. Some are quite cosy with fan-cooled cabins, electricity, and cold drinks. One of the popular expeditions leaves from Manaus. It sails up the Rio Negro to visit the Anavilhanas **Archipelago**. An archipelago is a group of islands.

The area around Manaus.

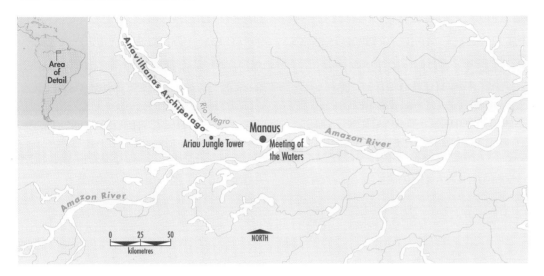

DID YOU KNOW?

Diseases are a real threat to rainforest visitors. Mosquitoes carry contagious diseases, such as yellow fever and malaria. Tourists can take a **vaccination** to prevent yellow fever. There is no vaccine for malaria. The best pre-vention is to avoid being bitten by mosqui-toes. Sleep inside a mosquito net at night. Wear long pants and long-sleeved shirts during the day. Use mosquito repellents.

The Anavilhana Islands are a nature reserve. There are small populations of jaguar, tapir, and manatee. The islands are a bird-watcher's paradise. There are astonishing numbers of orange-winged parrots and blue and yellow macaws. You may even see the rare harpy eagle in the emergent layer. As darkness falls, bats and birds of the night flutter around the boat.

A visit to a forest lodge or boat trip allows a tourist to see the unspoiled Amazon. Days are spent observing wildlife, taking photographs, or simply relaxing on white sand beaches. This is the best kind of tourism. Pho-tographs do not destroy the rainforest. Little damage is done to the animals or environ-ment. And the rainforest is protected for future generations to enjoy.

SOMETHING TO DO

1. Imagine you and your family are going to the Amazon on the holiday of a lifetime. You will be near Manaus for seven days. You may stay at a Jungle Tower or you may take a trip on the Amazonian Excursion riverboat. Write a diary describing your adventures to send back home to your classmates. Include sketches if you wish.

2. Hold a class discussion. Do you think "nature tourism" is a good idea for the Amazon? Explain.

3. Refer back to activity 4 in chapter 1, on page 3. Now that you have read more about the rainforest, would you change any items on your original list? Why?

Guests at the Ariau Jungle Tower often go on fishing expeditions. This boatload of tourists is fishing for piranhas, which are delicious when properly cooked.

s we saw in Chapter 3, South America is not the only continent that has a tropical rainforest. Large areas in Africa and Asia are also covered by rainforest.

The largest tropical rainforest in Africa is the basin of the Congo River. The whole area was once a huge shallow lake. Now it is the home of gorillas, chimpanzees, baboons, elephants, buffaloes, leopards, dwarf hippopotami, and many kinds of monkeys. Many species of birds, insects, and plants are found here though not as many as in the Amazon. It is also home for a race of small Aboriginal People.

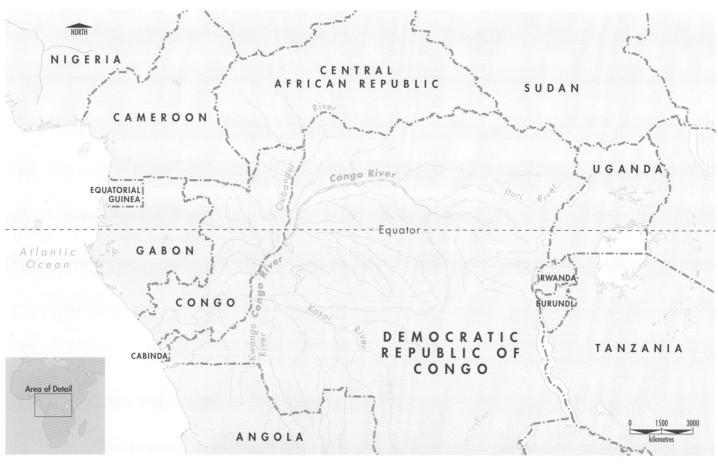

African elephants prefer to feed in clearings or along the edge of the forest. More than half their diet is leaves from trees, but elephants will travel deep into the rainforest to reach their favourite fruits.

The tropical rainforest of Africa is being cleared at an alarming rate. The best timber, such as mahogany, has been cut down and shipped overseas to make expensive furniture. The less valuable types of trees are made into plywood or chipboard. The frightening fact is that trees are being cut down faster than new ones can grow.

Huge areas of the rainforest have been cleared for another reason. They are cut down to make room for farms called plantations. Bananas, rubber, cacao, cotton, coffee, and oil palms are tropical crops that are grown on plantations.

COFFEE PLANTATIONS

Coffee is a plantation crop. Coffee trees came originally from Africa but they are now grown in several other places including Brazil. One plantation may have thousands of trees. Coffee trees are planted in rows but in the shade of taller trees.

The coffee berries are laid out in the sun to dry. After a few days, the beans can be taken out of the berry. Sometimes this is done by machine, but often it is done by hand. The coffee beans are dried, sorted, and packed in sacks. They are shipped all over the world. When the beans are roasted and ground, they are ready for making coffee.

When coffee trees are about four years old, they begin to produce berries. The berries are ripe when they turn cherry-red. They are picked by hand, which is back-breaking work. Inside each berry are two green seeds called the coffee beans.

OIL PALM PLANTATIONS

The oil palm grows wild in the tropical forests of West Africa. It is now grown on plantations there and in South Asia. The oil palm tree grows straight and tall. It has no branches but large feathery leaves grow from the top. It flowers and bears fruit between 12 and 20 times each year.

The fruits are cut off with a very sharp knife on the end of a long pole. When the fruit is split open there is a hard seed. Both the seed and the fleshy part of the fruit contain oil. The oil is collected and used to make soap, margarine, and candles. The indigenous people of West Africa use the oil for cooking and lighting.

An oil palm plantation in West Africa. Oil palm fruit appear in huge bunches. Each bunch weighs 15 to 20 kilograms.

SOMETHING TO DO

1. On an outline map of Africa label the Congo River and its tributaries. Mark the equator on the map. Shade in the tropical rainforests of that continent.

2. Draw a mural to show how coffee is produced. Start with a picture showing coffee growing on plantation trees. Finish with a steaming cup of coffee being served. Show each stage in between. Write a sentence or two under each picture to explain the process.

3. The coffee beans you see in the supermarket are dark brown. Find out what has turned them from green to brown.

24

The smallest people in the world live in the tropical rainforest of West Africa. One of these groups is the Mbuti people. They live in the deepest part of the forest, along the Ituri River.

The term **pygmy** is used to describe human populations in which the people are less than 1.5 metres tall. The Mbuti are pygmies. A fully grown man stands about 137 cm. An average Mbuti woman is about 131 cm.

They live in bands of six to 15 families. Each band has its own hunting area. Small bands hunt with bows and arrows. Large bands hunt with nets and spears. Net hunting requires the cooperation of the whole band, including women and children. Each man has a net; it is his most prized possession. It looks like a tennis net about 50 metres long, but this net is made of vines, twisted and knotted together. This kind of net needs frequent repair.

When an antelope, wild pig, or some other animal becomes entangled in the net, hunters rush forward with spears. The tip of each spear is coated with poison made from a rainforest plant. The animal is killed and the meat packed into the women's baskets. Everything from the hunt is shared. If a man or woman cannot hunt because of sickness or injury, their families receive a share anyway.

Occasionally Mbuti hunters kill an elephant. A group of hunters follow an elephant. When they get close enough, one hunter dashes forward and

The nets of the oldest hunters are strung between trees in an area where animals are thought to be. Each man attaches his net to the nets of his neighbours. The nets of the younger hunters are used to form a wide semicircle. The women and children walk towards the nets beating the ground, shouting and clapping their hands. They scare the game towards the nets.

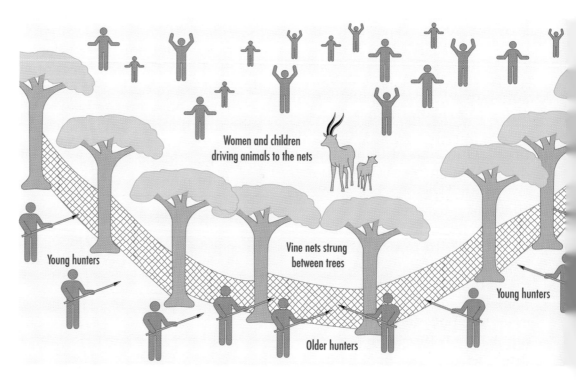

Women and children driving animals to the nets

Young hunters

Vine nets strung between trees

Young hunters

Older hunters

The Smallest People in the World

slashes the hamstring muscles behind the elephant's knees with a spear. Others thrust spears into the animal and leave the elephant to die. The next day the whole band returns to the dead animal. First they apologize to the spirit of the dead elephant. Then they cut it up and carry it back to the camp. Later they will trade the ivory tusks to the people who live at the edge of the forest.

Mbuti women pick berries, fruit, nuts, and the roots of certain plants and carry them back to camp in woven baskets. They also gather fallen branches for firewood and cook the meals over a fire in front of the hut.

When a band of Mbuti have lived in the same camp for three or four weeks, they find that most of the animals have been scared away. The amount of food they can gather has been reduced. So the Mbuti move on to a new campsite and build new shelters.

Almost everything the Mbuti require they find in the forest. The rest they obtain by trading with tribes who live on the edge of the rainforest. They exchange meat and honey for salt, tobacco, plantains, metal arrowheads, and spear points.

The Mbuti believe in **keti**. These are small invisible

creatures exactly like the Mbuti. If some little accident happens it is blamed on the keti. If a hunter trips, he says he bumped into a keti. If game is scarce it is because the keti hunted it first.

The Mbuti also believe that the rainforest is their friend who guides and protects them. They do not plant gardens and they do not cut down trees. In times of sickness or death, the Mbuti believe that the forest is sleeping. So to wake and cheer it up they hold a festival of singing and dancing. The main musical instruments are drums and a small tinkling instrument which they obtain by trade.

The women and girls make the huts. Mbuti huts are small, just big enough for one family. They are easily constructed in about one hour. Thin sticks are stuck in the ground. The ends are bent over and tied in the middle with vines. The whole structure is thatched with large leaves to keep out the rain. The photo shows a group of Mbuti children by a hut they have built. A family's hut is just like this, only bigger.

SOMETHING TO DO

1. In an organizer, compare the way of life of the Yanomami with the Mbuti. Use the following headings: animals hunted, methods of hunting, description of homes, how homes are built, how long the house lasts, foods gathered, crops grown, the role of women and children, the role of men, beliefs and superstitions.

2. Make a model of a Mbuti shelter as shown in the photograph. Try using drinking straws, plasticine, twigs, leaves, string and any other materials you can find.

25

Jungle is a Hindi word meaning dense forest and tangled undergrowth. It was first used to describe the rainforests of India. The mainland and the islands of tropical Asia were once covered with jungle or rainforest. Today much of the rainforest is disappearing. Trees have been cut down for timber and to make room for agriculture. Yet, the islands of South East Asia, such as Borneo and Sulawesi, still have large rainforests.

Rainforest
Former rainforest

The Dayak people live together in huge wooden houses called longhouses. Their houses have thatched roofs to keep out the rain. They are built on stilts above the ground to keep the floor dry. Often they are built right at the riverbank. Several families live in one house. Some houses hold several hundred people.

THE DAYAK PEOPLE OF BORNEO

Many different peoples live in the rainforests of South East Asia. The Dayak people are one of the tribes. They live on the island of Borneo, one of the thousands of islands that make up Indonesia. About one-tenth of the world's rainforest is found in Indonesia.

Dayak people find all their food and other needs in the forest. They collect fruits, roots, nuts, and shoots to eat. They are excellent hunters and are heavily armed. They use spears and blowpipes with poisoned arrows to kill monkeys, wild pigs, squirrels, lizards, and birds. Many also have dogs which they use in hunting. Fish are caught in the rivers with spears. These people hunt together and share all their food. When food becomes scarce in one area, the Dayaks move on. They choose another camp site and a new longhouse is built.

SOME RAINFOREST CREATURES

Borneo and the other islands are home to many rainforest creatures. Hundreds of different species of animals, birds, fish, and reptiles are found there. About 20 000 varieties of plants grow on these islands.

Orangutans live in the rainforests of Borneo and Sulawesi. They are **primates**—a group of mammals that includes monkeys, apes, and humans. Orangutans are large animals with a hairless face and small ears. They spend most of their time in the canopy looking for mangoes, figs, and other fruit. They also eat leaves and shoots. They have long strong arms for swinging through the trees. They are able to scoop up water and grip things in their large hands. At night they sleep in a nest of branches and leaves. Orangutans are an endangered species because of human hunters and the deforestation of their homeland.

RATTAN

Rattan is an important rainforest plant of South East Asia. Wild rattan palms climb their way up into the canopy using their spiny leaves and tendrils. Rattan is used to manufacture

cane furniture that is exported around the world. It is also made into baskets, fish traps, sleeping mats, hammocks, hats, walking sticks, and rope. The juice from the rattan fruit is used as a dye and a medicine for asthma, rheumatism, and snake bite.

Flying frogs live high up in the trees. Round suction cups on their fingers and toes help them to climb. They hunt for insects at night. To hide from enemies and to surprise their prey, the frogs lie on leaves that match the colour of their green bodies. Their large feet have long webbed toes. When they jump from tree to tree they spread out their webbed feet like parachutes. They glide through the air, travelling as far as 15 metres.

A rattan market in South East Asia. There are so many uses for rattan that it now costs more per tonne than many kinds of timber.

SOMETHING TO DO

1. Rainforest animals frequently use camouflage. In groups, find out and describe the camouflage of a creature from the Amazon rainforest and a creature from the rainforests of Asia. Try to choose different animals in each group. Draw pictures to illustrate the animals chosen.

2. In what ways are the homes of the Yanomami and the Dayak people similar? How are they different?

3. What is rattan? Why is this rainforest product so important?

26

*I*n the time it takes to read this paragraph, an area of tropical rainforest larger than an Olympic Games sports stadium will have been burned down, cut down with a chain saw, or knocked down with bulldozers. Every minute of every day somewhere in the world another area of rainforest disappears.

Slash and burn deforestation in the Amazon rainforest.

The rainforests of the world are in great danger. Everywhere they are being chopped down and destroyed. This is called **deforestation**. Today deforestation happens at a faster rate than ever before. Once a large area has been destroyed, the forest will probably never grow back again. What is left is a patch of dirt, overgrown with weeds.

WHY ARE RAINFORESTS DISAPPEARING?

Trees are being cut down for several reasons:
- to harvest timber for export and for firewood,
- to make space to raise cattle and to plant crops,
- to make room for settlers to build houses, towns, and farms,
- to carve roads through the rainforest,
- to construct huge hydroelectric dams and other industries, and
- to search for gold, copper, iron ore, lead, and diamonds.

WHY WE MUST SAVE THE RAINFOREST

If deforestation is not stopped soon, there will be serious consequences for our planet earth.

1. The rainforests will disappear. In a few years only West Africa and the Amazon basin will have any rainforest left. Once the trees have been removed, the soil has no protection. Rainfall will wash the surface soil away. We call this **erosion**. Once the surface soil erodes the land can't be used to grow anything for a long time.

2. If deforestation is not stopped, many animal and plant species will become **endangered** or close to dying out. When a species dies out, it is gone forever.

The rainforest is home to about half of the world's animal species. If their habitat disappears, the animals are doomed. For example, the jaguar needs a large area in which to hunt. As the forest shrinks, there will not be enough prey for the big cats. Jaguars will starve. Many will die and eventually the species will become extinct. What happens to the jaguar will happen to other rainforest creatures. Tigers, sloths, gorillas, and many birds and insects will disappear too.

Plants from rainforests provide us with many different foods and medicines. Many more might be waiting to be discovered. If we lose the rainforests, we will lose these future discoveries.

3. The disappearance of the rainforests threatens the way of life of the Aboriginal Peoples. The lands where forest people have always lived are being destroyed. The land is being used for roads, towns, farms, and ranches. Once the forest disappears, the tribes have no way of making their own living. They depend on the forest. They have nowhere else to go. They end up begging in the towns in order to stay alive.

4. If we destroy the rainforest, we destroy the environment. Trees purify the air we breathe. If too many trees are chopped down, the air in the forest changes. This affects the weather, even in countries thousands of kilometres away. Some scientists are concerned that if the huge tropical rainforests disappear, the whole of the earth's climate may change. Also, burning large areas of the rainforest affects the world's climate. Burning releases carbon dioxide, a poison gas, into the atmosphere. This contributes to the **greenhouse effect** where gases in the atmosphere trap heat. The earth's atmosphere heats up and causes all kinds of environmental problems including floods and drought.

Building roads through the Amazon rainforest can cause soil erosion. With nothing to hold it in place, the dirt on the roadside is washed away by heavy rains.

This is an Aboriginal child from the Amazon area in Brazil. She could see the surrounding rainforest disappear by the time she grows up.

SOMETHING TO DO

1. Design your own conservation poster to hang up on a school notice board. The design should give a message. It should tell about the importance of saving the rainforest, the plants or animals, the people or environment. Think of a clever heading for your poster to grab the attention of viewers. Design an illustration, or cut pictures out of magazines and make a collage.

onservationists are people who work to conserve and protect our environment. They have come up with some ideas for saving the rainforests.

IDEA FROM THE GOVERNMENT OF BRAZIL

Set Land Aside

Governments and conservation organizations have set aside sections of rainforest as protected zones. These have been marked out as "reserves" or "parks" for the Aboriginal Peoples. No one else is supposed to come into that territory. The tribes are able to lead their traditional lifestyle within its boundaries. In 1991 the government of Brazil set out a park for the Yanomami people.

IDEA FROM THE UNITED NATIONS

Biosphere Reserve

People at the United Nations have come up with this idea.

They call it the **Biosphere Reserve**. Here is how it works. Large areas of rainforests are set aside as protected zones. Strict conservation is practiced here. The inner core area is for plants and animals only. It cannot be disturbed. Surrounding the inner core are buffer zones. In zone one there can be scientific research and some forest people may live there. More rainforest people will live in zone 2. Aboriginal Peoples, rubber tappers, and caboclos will be allowed to hunt and to gather such products as rubber and Brazil nuts. But there will be no destruction of the rainforest. A small area in zones 1 and 2 will be open to nature tourism. A Biosphere Reserve shows one way for people to live in rainforests without destroying them.

IDEAS FROM THE FOREST PEOPLES' ALLIANCE

The Aboriginal Peoples of the Amazon have been forming organizations. The rubber tappers have joined them. The main organization is called the Forest Peoples' Alliance. They want to keep their land safe, protect their way of life, and make sure that the rainforest will be there for their children. Here are some of the ideas that the Alliance would like the government to adopt.

Core area

Buffer zone 1

Tourism Area

Buffer zone 2

Core area

Human settlement areas for food gathering, research and tourism

Research station

Rainforest peoples

Ideas for Protecting the Rainforest

A large gathering of Aboriginal Peoples met at Altamira, Brazil in 1989. They were protesting plans to build dams that would flood thousands of square kilometres of rainforest. As a result of this meeting, the government of Brazil stopped the project.

- No more rainforest should be destroyed for any reason.
- All big projects (roads, dams, new towns, and settlements) should be halted and alternatives found.
- The forest that is left should be protected. The parts that have been destroyed should be regrown. The knowledge that the indigenous forest people have should be put to good use. Science and technology should also be put to use.
- Special lands should be marked out for the rubber tappers, caboclos, and Aboriginal Peoples.
- Forest people should be allowed to take part in government.
- The settlers who are already in the forest should be shown how to live there without damaging it any more.

SOMETHING TO DO

1. In groups, evaluate each of the ideas suggested for saving the rainforests. Record your answers in an organizer. Use the problems we talked about in the last chapter as your questions or criteria. Explain the reasons for your answer.

   Questions to consider about the ideas:

   - Does this idea help to save the rainforest?
   - Does this idea help to protect rainforest plants and animals?
   - Does this idea help to protect the Aboriginal Peoples?
   - Does this idea help to save the earth's environment?
   - Would settlers, ranchers, and miners like this idea?
   - Would tourists like this idea?

CRITERIA	YES	NO	EXPLANATION

ou may think that there is nothing an ordinary person can do to help save the rainforest. You would be wrong. Thousands of students in all parts of the world have found ways. They take part in programs that allow them to "adopt" small pieces of rainforest.

These young people are collecting pop cans for recycling. With the money they raise, they will "adopt" a piece of rainforest.

Here is how the program works. For about $25, a group pays for the protection of an acre (about one-half hectare) of tropical rainforest for a year. The fee helps tropical countries to pay for urgent projects such as hiring and training forest rangers or researching ways to save a threatened species like the jaguar. Thousands of students from around the world have raised money to fund the "adoption" of a little piece of rainforest.

At the end of their study of the rainforest, one junior class decided they wanted to help. They came up with a list of specific things they could do to help save the rainforest. Here is their list:

THINGS WE CAN DO TO HELP THE RAINFOREST.

1. Do not keep exotic wild pets such as parrots, snakes, and lizards if they were collected in the wild.

2. Do not buy animal skins, ivory, coral, or souvenir sea shells.

3. Do not buy goods made out of tropical hardwoods.

4. Tell others about the problems of the rainforest.

5. Join a nature conservation group such as the World Wildlife Fund.

6. Buy or sponsor a tree for somebody as a birthday or anniversary present.

7. Raise money to adopt a small piece of a tropical rainforest.

What Can We Do to Help?

One Survival International project is to provide solar-powered radios for Aboriginal Peoples. The aim is to inform tribal peoples about the struggles and victories of others who face the same problems. By radio broadcasts, people who do not read and have no electricity can keep in touch with matters of urgent concern to them.

SOURCES OF INFORMATION

Listed below are some organizations involved in conserving the rainforest. Conservation organizations offer opportunities for you to get involved in trying to save the rainforest and its inhabitants.

**World Wildlife Fund
90 Eglinton Ave. East
Suite 504
Toronto, Ontario, M4P 2Z7
Tel. 416-489-8800**

The WWF works to protect endangered species, endangered places, and tropical forests. A special school subscription provides teaching packs, brochures, posters, and ideas for school children.

**Survival International
11-15 Emerald Street,
London WC 1N 3QL
England.**

Survival International has projects all over the world to support people like the Yanomami. They do a lot of work in the Amazon. They produce newsletters, books, and gift products to support tribal people.

DID YOU KNOW?

James Park Elementary School in British Columbia held a toy sale to raise money to adopt six acres of tropical rainforest. Children at Kew Beach Public School in Toronto, held a "Love For The World" Valentine's Day bake sale and donated all the proceeds to the rainforest.

SOMETHING TO DO

1. Think about the list that the junior class came up with to help the rainforest. Are there other suggestions you can add? Add them to their list. Then join three partners and discuss all the ideas you have on your lists. Which are the best ideas? Rank all the ideas in order of importance. Number one is the best idea. Be able to explain your ranking to other groups.

2. Write to a conservation organization to find out how your class can help the rainforest and its animals.

3. Write a short play about a day in the life of one of the tropical rainforest tribes. Try to show some of the problems facing the Aboriginal Peoples. Ask your friends to help you perform the play. Can you find an audience in the community to watch your play? Perhaps you could raise money from your performance to protect the rainforest.

Glossary

Aboriginal Peoples people whose ancestors have lived in an area for thousands of years.

archipelago a group of islands.

basin an area of land that supplies a river with water.

Biosphere Reserve a United Nations plan to set aside large areas of the rainforest as nature reserves with special zones set aside for plants and animals, for indigenous peoples, and for limited tourism.

bolos a huge ball of raw rubber.

bromeliads plants that catch water by using their leaves as containers.

buttress root a large root, a portion of which grows above ground to support an unusually tall tree.

caboclos a mixed race of people descended from Portuguese settlers and Aboriginal Peoples.

camouflage the colouring of animals that allows them to blend in with their background.

carnivores meat eaters.

conservationist a person who works for preservation of the natural environment.

curare a powerful poison made from bark or roots of certain trees or vines.

deforestation the process of cutting down and destroying an area of forest.

endangered in danger of dying out.

enzymes chemicals that help to digest food.

epiphytes plants that anchor themselves to trunks and branches of trees.

equator an imaginary line around the middle of the earth.

erosion what takes place when rainfall washes away the surface soil.

evergreens trees that keep their leaves all year round.

fertile describes soil that is good for growing crops.

flood plain an area that floods regularly.

flying frogs frogs that can use their webbed feet as parachutes in jumping from tree to tree.

food chain the order in which animals eat other animals or plants.

genipapo a tree used to make a black dye for body decoration.

greenhouse effect occurs when gases in the atmosphere trap heat, causing the earth's atmosphere to heat up.

habitat the natural home of plants and animals.

herbivores plant eaters.

hygrometer an instrument that measures the amount of humidity in the air.

jungle a Hindi word meaning dense forests and tangled undergrowth.

jute a crop grown on flood plains and used to make burlap.

keti invisible people believed by the Mbuti people to cause accidents.

latex milky, white sap found in the rubber tree.

legend on a map or chart, the words that give the meanings of the symbols used.

legends stories passed down to explain how the world was created or why certain things happen.

lianas thick, woody vines.

manioc the root of a plant used by the Yanomami to make bread.

mouth the place where a river flows into the sea.

nature tourism a way for tourists to see and explore the environment without destroying it.

nocturnal active at night.

orangutan a large mammal with a hairless face and small ears living in the rainforests of South East Asia.

parrot a colourful bird of the rainforest.

peixada a stew made of fish from the Amazon River.

plantain a fruit like a large banana that is used for cooking.

plantations huge farms.

plaza the open space in the middle of a yano.

precipitation rain or snowfall.